This journal belongs to:

_____

D1088692

Five Minutes in the Morning

A FOCUS JOURNAL

ASTER*

An Hachette UK Company
www.hachette.co.uk

First published in Great Britain in 2017 by Aster, a division of
Octopus Publishing Group Ltd
Carmelite House
50 Victoria Embankment
London EC4Y 0DZ
www.octopusbooks.co.uk

ISBN 978-1-91202-301-1

A CIP catalogue record for this book is available from the British Library.

Printed and bound in China

25 24 23 22 21 20

MIX
Paper from
responsible sources
FSC® C008047

CONTENTS

INTRODUCTION
FIVE
MINUTES
IN THE
MORNING

Try this experiment today, or first thing tomorrow morning. Set a timer for five minutes, find somewhere quiet and comfortable to sit, where you won't be distracted, and just sit for five minutes. Just breathe and allow your thoughts to come, watch them, just an observer for these few minutes...

... how did those five minutes feel? Did it feel like a surprising amount of time when all you had to do was sit? Was it hard to sit still when you have so many things to be getting on with?

This journal is the gift of giving yourself these few minutes at the beginning of the day for a little self-enquiry and reflection. How are you? What do you need today? What is your intention for the day ahead?

Instead of rushing headlong into the day ahead, when you give yourself space to settle for a few moments, you take that feeling with you. You might simply look out of the window and notice the world around you, or check in with your goals for this year and what you need to progress them. You'll be amazed at what a difference these few minutes may begin to make to the rest of your day.

The theme of this journal is "focus". Focus on you, focus on your life and focus on achieving your dreams and desires. Most of the short exercises use writing to explore the theme, while some simply require your attention. To begin with, there are exercises to help clear the way, as so often it is ourselves who are in our own way. All that mental clutter, all those worries, fears and doubts. In the pages ahead are simple ways to identify, accept and release, so that we may feel the open spaces of our hearts and minds again.

In the second section of the journal, you can explore what really matters to you – it's time to put those things and people back at the top of the list. The third section will develop your attitude of abundance – celebrating what is good in your life and inviting more of what you wish for. There are then exercises that explore obstacles and challenges and how you can practise new ways of approaching these – through creativity, seeing things differently, tapping into your subconscious or playing games.

And the final section of the journal and the focus journey offers exercises to help supercharge your levels of productivity and reach those goals, not always by doing more, but often by choosing how to do less. The journal is designed so that you can either use the pages to write on freely or you can write in your own notebook. Some days you may wish to simply open the journal to a random page and see what's there, or you can work through the process. Make a note of which exercises resonate most with you as these will give you a personal toolkit for developing your own daily focus habits and rituals.

THE POWER
OF WRITING

The very act of writing something down gives shape to our thoughts. Seeing an idea or feeling set out on paper gives us a new perspective and can help us to be more objective. Perhaps that idea we've been pondering really does have potential, or the worry we've been carrying is not so serious after all.

Writing helps us to clear our minds. If we get the list of things we have to do out of our heads and onto paper, then our brains will have space for more important thoughts.

Words bring our thoughts to life, so committing our goals to paper makes it more likely that we will achieve them. The same is true for our hopes and desires.

So grab a pen and remember, what you write is for your eyes only.

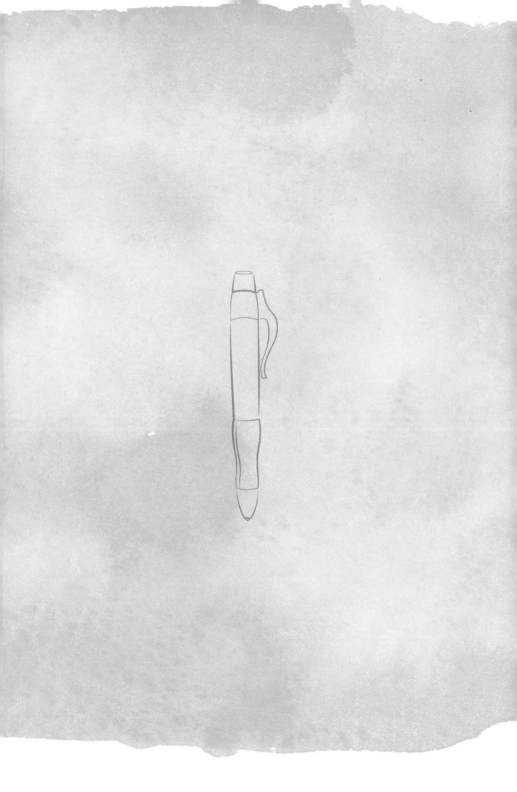

AN EXERCISE TO START WRITING

A blank page can be intimidating so don't think,
just write your name.

Now try to imagine you are meeting yourself for the first
time and write down how you would introduce yourself.
Don't read it back, don't correct as you go, just keep writing
until you run out of things to say and then stop.

Do it again tomorrow, and the next day and the day after that,
each time starting from where you left off, until spending five
minutes in the morning writing becomes a habit.

WRITE A LOVE LETTER TO YOURSELF

Self-confidence is a vital ingredient of both our own happiness and, because happiness is contagious, the happiness of those closest to us. But when was the last time you gave yourself a pat on the back, or looked in the mirror and told yourself that you liked what you saw? Writing a love letter to yourself might sound odd (we are rarely encouraged to praise ourselves, after all), but setting out all the things you are proud of and the attributes you admire is a great way to boost your self-esteem.

If you find it hard to get started, imagine that you are writing about your best friend. Think about why s/he is your friend and which of her/his characteristics you value most.

I FEEL MOST ENERGIZED WHEN...

Write a list of all the things you do and the people you see on a regular basis and put a tick by the energy boosters. These are the positive influences in your life so seek them out, especially when you are feeling drained or uninspired.

Now think about the activities and people you haven't ticked – do any of them actually sap your energy and bring you down? If the answer is "yes", what can you do to change the situation?

DESCRIBE ONE
OF THE BEST
MOMENTS OF
YOUR LIFE

"Life isn't a matter of milestones,
but of moments."

ROSE FITZGERALD KENNEDY

Noticing the good things in our lives encourages us to think positively and positive thinking has been proven to be good for both our health and our happiness.

Use the space below to relive one of your best moments.

STREAM OF CONSCIOUSNESS

This exercise is like a spring-clean for the mind.

Find a quiet, comfortable spot where you won't
be disturbed and get some paper and a pen.
Set a timer for five minutes.

Now write down everything and anything that comes
into your head. (If you can't think of anything, write
"I can't think of anything.")

When the alarm goes, stop and walk away from your
paper without looking at it.

Do something else for five minutes, then come back
and read what you wrote, paying attention to any
recurring themes.

Finally, destroy the piece of paper – this will reassure
you that no one will ever read what you wrote and that
will give you the confidence to write freely.

Repeat whenever you feel stressed or anxious.

TODAY...

Here are some more writing prompts you can choose
from any day you feel stuck for words.

Today I am most grateful for...

Today I wish for...

Today what I really need is...

Today I am going to...

Today I feel...

HOW DO YOU REALLY FEEL?

"The cure for pain is in the pain."

RUMI

When we put our feelings into words, studies show that we become less attached to them and more able to live in the present without distraction. Just by labeling our emotions, we help our brain to process them. And by engaging in this process you are also allowing yourself to truly feel, rather than suppress any difficult emotion. As soon as you acknowledge a feeling it immediately releases its grip.

Stop for a moment and properly consider how you are feeling right now. Jot those feelings down and read them back to yourself. Allow yourself to take pleasure from the positive feelings you have expressed.

Now think about the negative ones. Don't judge them – this isn't about "good" versus "bad" – just acknowledge their presence and ask yourself why you are you experiencing those feelings.

CLEARING THE WAY

Everything feels better when our minds are clear. In fact, you could argue that having a clear mind is essential to our sense of positive wellbeing since mental clarity makes us feel more energized and more in control of our lives, thus reducing stress and enabling us to make better decisions.

Achieving clarity isn't difficult but it does require conscious effort, so the next few pages are filled with ideas, suggestions and exercises all designed to help clear the way.

TAKE NOTICE

*"The true secret of happiness
lies in taking a genuine interest
in all the details of daily life."*

WILLIAM MORRIS

Mindfulness is a mental state of being in which you focus on the present moment and simply take notice. It is a state of awareness in which you are able to notice and acknowledge what is going on both inside you and in your surroundings.

Here are three simple exercises to draw your attention to the small but important elements that make up your everyday life:

1 When you wake up, stay in bed and spend five minutes just looking at your bedroom. Notice the pictures on the wall, the pieces of furniture and the way the light filters through the curtains.

2 Go out into the garden, stand on the balcony or just open a window. Close your eyes and listen to the sounds of the morning.

3 Make yourself a cup of coffee and take five minutes to drink it. Do nothing else, simply be aware of how the cup feels in your hand, breathe in the aroma and savour the taste.

THREE DEEP BREATHS

Next time you have a few minutes spare, don't check your phone; take three deep breaths instead and, as you do so, concentrate on nothing but the feel of the air as it comes into and then leaves your body with each breath. Notice the sensation in your nostrils, shoulders and rib cage.

Another great way to clear your mind for the day ahead is to find a noun for each letter of the alphabet, or a city or even a food (although this might just make you really hungry).

BRAIN DUMPING

Computers work best when there aren't too many applications running in the background. The same is true of our brains; an overload of thoughts will clog them up and slow them down.

Clearing out our brains is known as a "brain dump" and it's easy: all you have to do is take five minutes to write down every single thing that's in your head, from concerns about the state of the world to the groceries you need to buy for tonight's supper.

Once all those thoughts are down on paper, rather than in your head, your brain will have space to do what it does best – work stuff out – and once you can see the clutter laid out before you, you can start to sort it.

Remember, less clutter = more clarity.

CLEAR THE CLUTTER

"Out of clutter, find simplicity."

ALBERT EINSTEIN

A tidy house may not always reflect a tidy mind but it is certainly true that, for many of us, a too-cluttered physical world can become a reflection of our mental one. Overflowing cupboards and surfaces buried under piles of papers often make us feel as though our heads are a chaotic mess too.

The solution is, of course, to clear the clutter.

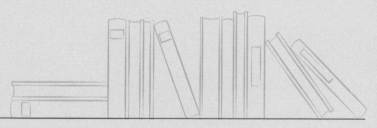

AN EXERCISE FOR PHYSICAL TIDYING

If the idea of one Herculean clear-out feels overwhelming,
try a series of small ones instead – starting today.

Pick a surface in your home.

Set a timer for five minutes, and tidy until the alarm goes off.
If you have time, give the surface a wipe and a polish too.

Repeat with a new surface tomorrow.

I COULD NEVER...

*"Fear kills more
dreams than
failure ever will."*

SUZY KASSEM

There's nothing wrong with not wanting to do certain things,
but every so often we should take a look at what we're not
doing and ask ourselves why.

Divide the page into two columns. In the first column make a list of all the things you think you could never do, then write the reason why opposite. Go back and look at it at regular intervals. Think about your justifications – are they really valid or simply excuses?

_____   _____

_____   _____

_____   _____

_____   _____

_____   _____

_____   _____

_____   _____

_____   _____

_____   _____

_____   _____

_____   _____

_____   _____

_____   _____

_____   _____

FEEL YOUR FEARS

"Fear is only as deep as the mind allows."

JAPANESE PROVERB

We are hardwired to feel fear – it's what keeps us safe, after all – but most of us are also prone to inappropriate fears; fear of failure, fear of speaking in public, fear of leaving a bad relationship, whether personal or professional. Inappropriate fears have no positive purpose and the first step to overcoming them is to know what they are. Make a list of everything you're afraid of and, as you name your fears, think about how they make your feel.

The process of setting your fears down on paper will help clarify
your thinking and allow you to look at them more objectively,
almost as if those fears belonged to somebody else.

WHAT IS STOPPING YOU?

Mental blocks hold us back from doing the things that we really want to do. Replacing "I know I can't" with "perhaps I can" is one way of clearing the blocks and allowing the positive energy to flow.

Write down five things that you think you can't do, along with the reasons why.

Now rewrite the list, swapping the negative words for positive ones. For example:

"I can't apply for that job because I don't meet all the criteria" becomes
"I can apply for that job because I have most of the skills they ask for."

Read through the positive list (aloud ideally) and see how it feels.

CLEARING RESISTANCE

"Every day holds the possibility of a miracle."

ELIZABETH DAVID

It doesn't always feel like this. You might even be resisting or rejecting these words right now. It's often easier to resist than to step into the unknown of possibility, to feel almost comfortable in our limitations – better to doubt our abilities than make fools of ourselves trying.

And yet deep down you know the falsity of this way of thinking. Your spirit of adventure and your courage are there and, even if resistance has thrown water on the flames, there is still a spark or a glow waiting to be brought back to life.

For these few minutes simply describe your life in flow. What does it look like? How does it feel? There are no boundaries here – go wherever you wish. Go with the flow.

LETTING GO

"Let go or be dragged."

ZEN PROVERB

We need to learn to let go of negative thoughts and old grievances because they simply clutter up our minds and drain our mental energy. There are many reasons that we cling to things, thoughts or people that no longer serve us. Sometimes it might simply be out of habit, or a desire to be proved right. Other times the thought of letting go seems harder than holding on. But the consequences are that you may feel stuck and that rather than going with the flow of life you are fighting against the current.

Think of your mind as a filing cabinet. Like their physical counterparts, the drawers of these mental storage systems need to be sorted through and cleared out on a regular basis.

Imagine yourself opening the drawers. Take out each thought in turn and ask yourself, "Does this thought contribute to my sense of wellbeing?" If the answer is "no", then you need to let it go. (It might help to write the thought down on a piece of paper so you can physically crumple it up and throw it away.)

FOCUS ON
WHAT MATTERS

Do you ever find yourself rushing from one
place to the next or between tasks? Do you feel
as though there just aren't enough hours in the
day to even get halfway through your to-do list?
The scatter-gun approach is never going to work;
it's time to focus on what really matters to you.

THE BIG PICTURE

"This too shall pass."

TRADITIONAL ADAGE

It is all too easy to blow our day-to-day anxieties out of proportion
and lose our sense of perspective. Next time you feel this starting
to happen, try to think about the problem from the point of view of
your future self. Imagine yourself in a year's time – how much will
the wrangle with your boss, the forthcoming presentation or the
argument with your partner matter then?

Try this manifestation exercise. Choose an aspect of your life, for example your career, finances or relationship. Now spend five minutes imagining all the detail of how you wish that aspect of your life to feel. Create a vibrant mental picture and really begin to lean in and experience how it feels.

LISTEN – AND BE RECEPTIVE TO WHAT YOU HEAR

"Listen to the wind, it talks.
Listen to the silence, it speaks.
Listen to your heart, it knows."

NATIVE AMERICAN PROVERB

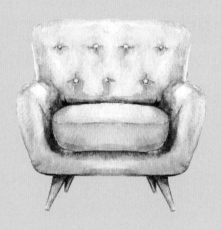

Humans are intuitive, but most of us have forgotten how to listen so that we really hear what our bodies and minds are telling us.

Receptive listening requires stillness and silence, so go somewhere you won't be disturbed and that is free from distractions and take five minutes to just sit and take notice of how you are feeling right now.

Go through each part of your body in turn, listen to what it is telling you and be open to what you hear. (Perhaps your jaw is tense. That is a common a sign of stress. Take notice.)

Repeat often.

WHAT DO YOU DESIRE?

"Far away in the sunshine are my highest aspirations. I cannot reach them: but I can look up, and see their beauty, believe in them, and try to follow where they lead."

LOUISA MAY ALCOTT

Listing our hopes and dreams makes it more likely that they will come true. Why? Because seeing them set down on paper helps to clarify what they are and that, in turn, enables us to work out what we need to do to realize them.

Divide your desires into work-based ones and emotional ones. Don't limit yourself – a wish list of desires is no place for realism. Just write down what, in an ideal world, you would most love to happen.

DISCOVER YOUR "WHY?"

In the previous exercise, you explored and expressed your desires. Look at that list and choose one of these wishes. Write it again and underneath, write "Why?" Ask yourself this question, listen deeply to what your heart replies and write down the answer. Then ask yourself again, "Why?" Continue this inquiry for a few minutes, and if you get to the heart of the desire, feel free to explore the next.

Look at your answers. Are you surprised at all at where they have taken you? Perhaps they have opened up a new level of knowing that may nourish you as you take steps toward your goals and desires.

_____

_____

_____

_____

_____

_____

_____

_____

_____

_____

_____

_____

_____

_____

_____

VALUES

"I think curiosity is our friend that teaches us how to become ourselves."

ELIZABETH GILBERT

We are told that living in accordance with our core values will make us happier and more fulfilled. But what exactly are our values?

Look at where you are in your life right now and ask yourself the question "What matters to me most?"

Write down the first five things (love, family, adventure, contribution, recognition etc.) that come into your head and then rank them 1–5, with 1 being the most important. These are your core values.

Put the list somewhere you will see it regularly and stop for a moment each day to consider whether your behaviour is helping you to realize your core values. For example, if a close family life is one of your core values then your habits should reflect that, which means not bringing work home at the weekend or checking your email on holiday.

WHAT ARE YOUR STRENGTHS?

Acknowledging what we do well boosts our self-confidence and makes it more likely that we will succeed. Here are some tips to help you identify what you are good at:

- Ask the people close to you to name three things they think you are good at. Believe what they tell you.

- Think about the times when you feel most capable and empowered – what skills are you using? Those are things you are good at.

- Go over the challenges you've faced in life and think about how you overcame them. Is there a common theme? If so, that is something you are good at too.

- What did you do that made you stand out as a child? You may not do it any more, but you still possess that talent.

Spend five minutes this morning listing your strengths and talents. What are you good at? Don't be bashful.

CHOOSE
YOUR GOALS

Goals might not sound like much fun but they breathe life into your dreams, they keep you moving forward rather than getting stuck in a rut. Goals are an important focus tool because they give you a clear target to aim at and a sense of direction or a map with which to get there. Goals can also be very effective in overcoming procrastination and getting to the finishing line when it comes to important tasks.

Of course, life often takes us in a slightly different direction than the one we set out on, so you don't need to be dogged in your pursuit of a goal to the point where you forget to look up or around as you go on your journey. Use the energy and impetus that goals offer.

Now that you have explored your dreams, desires, values and strengths, you can trust your instincts to select between three and five things to do this year. Don't think about it too hard, be guided by what speaks to you most clearly.

SUCCESSFUL GOAL SETTING

"Well begun is half done."

ARISTOTLE

Having goals is part of being human, even though the path toward our goals might not always run in a smooth or very straight line. Goals are lined with our sense of meaning and purpose and how engaged we feel. We don't have to be rigidly attached to the goal outcomes but they can certainly help keep us focused and moving forward.

123

Before you set any goal, ask yourself these three questions:

1 What do I really want?

2 Why do I want it?

3 What actions do I need to take?

ALIGNMENT OF GOALS AND VALUES

We are more likely to achieve our goals if they align with our core values.

Jot down your 3-5 goals from the previous exercise. Opposite these, write your list of core values. Draw a line between all those that connect. Now consider the stray goals. Can you adjust them so that they will correspond with your values? If not, ask yourself why you have set yourself this goal. If it doesn't speak to your values, what will achieving it add to your life?

GOALS

VALUES

_____

_____

_____

_____

_____

_____

_____

_____

_____

_____

_____

_____

_____

_____

_____

_____

_____

_____

STEPPING STONES

"The man who removes a mountain begins by carrying away small stones."

CHINESE PROVERB

Now that you have identified your big goals, you need to break them down into a series of achievable steps. The smaller the better. (You can always take them two at a time.)

Write your end goal at the top of the page then, in a sentence, state how you are going achieve it.

Now start to make a list of what that will actually involve day to day. For example, say your goal is to lose weight and you plan to do it by eating better and moving more. The day-to-day list will be full of mini goals such as: Monday, take the stairs instead of the lift; Tuesday, take salad in for lunch rather than buying a sandwich; Wednesday, run/walk for at least 20 minutes after work.

Keep your eyes on the next step rather than constantly gazing up at the summit.

YOUR MISSION
STATEMENT

"To be a teacher. And to be known for inspiring my students to be more than they thought they could be."

OPRAH WINFREY'S PERSONAL MISSION STATEMENT

In *The 7 Habits of Highly Effective People*, Stephen R Covey introduced the idea that individuals as well as companies could benefit from writing a personal mission or purpose statement. This is a short statement that encapsulates how you wish to live your life, the contribution you wish to make and to whom.

Sit for five minutes and take this time to re-cap the previous few exercises in which you have visualized your big picture, named your desires and explored your values and strengths. In a free-flowing style, now just write whatever comes to you as your personal mission statement.

FOCUS ON ABUNDANCE

If we spend all our time focused on what's lacking in our lives we will never be content. However, if we shift our perspective and begin to think about all that we do have, everything changes. Approaching the day ahead from a position of abundance rather than scarcity helps us to live life more fully.

INVITE ENERGY

Energy is all around us. You can feel the energy as you walk into a room of people, some mornings you wake up full of positive energy, while on others you might feel that your batteries are close to running on empty.

Energy creates energy, it is a virtuous circle, so we should all try to start the day by inviting energy into our bodies and minds.

Here are some things to try. Pick one for today:

- Make a playlist of music that lifts your spirits and listen to something from it each morning as you are getting up. Sing along, have a dance.

- Open out your body with a stretch or two.

- Go outside and stand on the grass in your bare feet.

- Open the window, breathe deeply and let the air in.

AFFIRMATIONS

Affirmations are positive statements, spoken aloud, about who you are and your place in the world. Here are some examples:

I am in control of my own life. I know my path.

I have a loving family and friends who support me.

Today is going to be a good day, filled with joy.

I allow myself to be happy and share my happiness with others.

I choose to be proud of myself.

Make a list of your own affirmations and speak them aloud
each morning to flood your brain with positive thoughts.

PLANTING THE SEEDS OF YOUR INTENTIONS

Find a quiet space and sit or lie down.

Take a minute to focus on your breathing – count your breaths in and out.

Now imagine that you are walking into a garden. Hear the birds, notice the flowers and the trees. There is a bag of seeds in your hand. These are the seeds of your intentions, your hopes and goals. Kneel down and begin to plant the seeds in the warm soil. Water them and bless them for containing everything they need to grow and fulfil their potential.

Sit in the garden for a moment before bringing your attention slowly back to your breathing. Count your breaths in and out and then open your eyes.

Return to your garden for five minutes each morning to water your seeds and watch them grow. If any stop growing, or fail to appear, simply plant that particular seed again.

VISUALIZE THE FUTURE

Visualizing is a way to "create" your own future in your imagination in such a way that you actually make it more likely to happen. It isn't about trying to control or fix the future, or being attached to only one possible outcome, it is about becoming open to experiences and feelings and allowing life to flow.

Here is an exercise for Monday morning to help you avoid that "where on earth did the time go?" feeling.

Imagine that it is already Friday.

Now write down three things that you are proud to have achieved during the week. Turning what you have imagined into reality is your vision for the week ahead.

BEGIN YOUR VISION BOARD

It can be easier to understand an intention such as "I would like to be calmer" if you can see what "calmer" actually looks like. A vision board is simply a visual display designed to draw your attention to your goals and intentions.

Begin today by making a list of your personal and professional aims and then list the type of images, photographs, quotations etc. that will remind you of your aims, inspire you to achieve them and reassure you that you are already on the right track. Even better, find a couple of those images right away and begin your vision board, putting it somewhere you will see it every day.

ACCEPTANCE

"…the best thing one can do
when it is raining, is to let it rain."

HENRY WADSWORTH LONGFELLOW,
TALES OF A WAYSIDE INN

In psychological terms, acceptance is our ability to acknowledge
a situation without protest or making any attempt to change it.
Acceptance is not about passivity and opting out, it is about
recognizing which aspects of our lives are beyond our control.
Many of us struggle to come to terms with difficult or painful
events, but exploring the positive things that have come
out of them can make the process easier.

Think of something you are finding difficult to accept and write for five minutes about everything you've done since that you would not have done otherwise. For example, if your relationship hadn't ended, you wouldn't have gone on that trip to Japan because your ex hated flying; or if you had got that promotion, you wouldn't have had so much time to spend with your children while they were small.

GRATITUDE

"Feeling gratitude and not expressing it is like wrapping a present and not giving it."

WILLIAM ARTHUR WARD

Expressing gratitude boosts our sense of wellbeing because it draws our attention to all the good things we have in our lives, filling us with positive energy.

The next set of exercises is designed to help you notice all the positive things life offers.

Spend five minutes this morning thinking about and writing down everything you have to be grateful for in the day ahead. It could be as simple as the sunshine, the fact that you have a job to go to, the food in your refrigerator or the wi-fi that means you can speak to your friend on the other side of the world.

WHAT WENT WELL YESTERDAY?

"Optimism is a choice."

ROY T BENNETT, *THE LIGHT IN THE HEART*

It can feel strange at first to find ways to praise yourself, it's often easier to focus on what you haven't achieved rather than the things you have. There might be a worry that this feels a short step away from arrogance or self-satisfaction.

Put these conditioned thoughts aside for today and give yourself five minutes to reflect on everything you did manage to achieve yesterday. If you make this reflection a daily habit then you can begin to build up momentum in certain areas and before you know it, you'll be on a streak.

Big or small, write it down and allow yourself to be proud.

_____

_____

_____

_____

_____

_____

_____

_____

_____

_____

_____

_____

_____

_____

_____

WHAT IS
YOUR STORY?

Feeling that we are in control of our lives plays an important role in our sense of wellbeing. However, it's all too easy for the pressures of everyday life to pile up to such an extent that events appear to be controlling us, rather than vice versa. One way we can help reverse the situation is to turn the coming day's events into a series of stories in which we are the hero.

For example, if you have a presentation to do at work, write a few sentences describing how well you do it, the techniques you use to successfully engage your audience and the clever way you respond to their questions. Or perhaps you are hosting a family get-together; write a five-minute story about how delicious the food is and the relaxed way in which you negotiate the usual family tensions.

WHO IS
IMPORTANT
TO YOU?

"You just stay here in this one corner of the Forest waiting for the others to come to you. Why don't you go to them sometimes."

A A MILNE, *THE HOUSE AT POOH CORNER*

Spend five minutes this morning making a list of all the people you would go to when you need a shoulder to cry on or someone to share your joy.

INSPIRATION

Find a saying, a poem or a piece of prose that speaks to you and fires your imagination. Write it down and look at it often.

_____

_____

_____

_____

_____

_____

_____

_____

_____

_____

_____

_____

_____

_____

_____

_____

WHAT DO YOU WONDER ABOUT?

"Wonder is the beginning of wisdom."

SOCRATES

Allowing yourself time to wonder and let your imagination roam free is a very special gift than you can give to yourself. It's ironic because "focus" suggests that you need to be laser-like in your focus to get things done. Like most things in life, it is a question of balance. When you have a specific task in front of you and you know what needs to be done, being narrow in your focus and giving it all your attention will get it completed quickly and efficiently. But there are also times when opening up your mind to the big questions will open you up to the wonder and magic that is in life, too, and this will infuse your everyday focus with meaning and curiosity.

Curiosity may have killed the cat but it is what drives humans forward. Ask who, what, when, where and how every day.

FOCUS ON PROBLEM SOLVING

We can't always avoid problems but we can get better at solving them. Sometimes our mind needs to be woken up, while other times we break the problem down into manageable steps or we can even tap into the power of the subconscious mind.

RECOGNIZE THE PROBLEM

Before you can begin to solve a problem, you need to recognize its existence, which is often easier to see in others than ourselves. Practising awareness is the first important step, or in other words paying attention.

Here are some ways to help you recognize that a problem exists:

You feel frustrated.

You keep having the same conversation repeatedly.

You know that something has to change.

You begin to see a pattern and wish to break out.

Spend five minutes paying attention to any areas of your day or life that bring you frustration, where it feels like the same patterns are happening over and over. Just observe them and begin to raise your awareness around the problem.

_____

_____

_____

_____

_____

_____

_____

_____

_____

_____

_____

_____

_____

_____

_____

_____

_____

ASK "WHY?" TO IDENTIFY THE PROBLEM

"He who has a why to live for can bear almost any how."

FRIEDRICH NIETZSCHE

You might think the problem is that you're stressed all the time, but it's not. Stress is just a symptom. If you are going to find a cure for the stress, you have to find out what's causing it in the first place and one of the best ways to do that is to keep asking yourself "why?"

Begin by writing down the problem ("I am always stressed", for example), then write down why; perhaps "I am overwhelmed by the number of things I have to do."

Now ask yourself "why?" again and write that answer down – maybe you think it's because you don't get any help at home or at work. But that is likely to be a symptom of something else too so, once again, ask yourself "why?"

Keep going until you have asked "why?" at least five times.

DRAW A PICTURE AND TAKE IT ONE STEP AT A TIME

Some problems are too large to be solved in one fell swoop. Setting down all the different causes of a problem helps you to find a solution one step at a time.

Try drawing a fishbone diagram (also known as an Ishikawa diagram) like this:

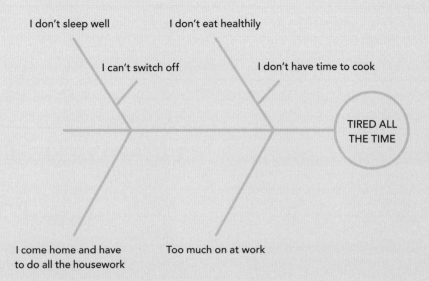

I don't sleep well

I don't eat healthily

I can't switch off

I don't have time to cook

TIRED ALL THE TIME

I come home and have to do all the housework

Too much on at work

Begin by writing the problem on the right-hand side of your paper and draw a box around it.

Now draw a horizontal line (the fish's "back bone") across the page with several smaller lines branching off it. Each of these "bones" represents a main cause.

Those causes have causes of their own so draw more lines, one for each sub-cause. Keep going until you have exhausted all possible causes.

Finally, take a step back and look at what you have drawn. Your solution to the big problem lies in the answers to all those small sub-causes, which you can deal with one at a time.

QUESTIONS AND ANSWERS

Begin by asking yourself these three questions:

What is the current situation that's causing me a problem?

What would I like the situation to be?

What is standing in my way?

Now write down your answers to each one (we have used exhaustion as an example). Stick to the facts and be specific:

I am exhausted.

I would like to have more energy.

I have too much to do when I get home so there is no time to relax and get to bed early.

Now think of one change you can make that will have the
biggest impact on improving your situation.

_____

_____

_____

_____

_____

_____

_____

_____

_____

_____

_____

_____

_____

_____

_____

LOOK AT THINGS
DIFFERENTLY

If you were to imagine yourself standing on the left of the image below, what number would you see? Now imagine standing on the right – do you still see the same number?

If you have been looking at an issue from the same perspective over and over, write it down and spend a couple of minutes looking at it from an alternative view. Do you see anything differently now?

TAP INTO YOUR SUBCONSCIOUS MIND

Even when your conscious mind feels completely stuck with a problem, your subconscious mind will continue to work on it without you even realizing. This is why eureka moments so often happen when you are relaxed, while you're in the shower, for example, or enjoying a walk and not really thinking about anything.

You can tap into this incredible resource of experience, knowledge, creativity and intuition when you need to, especially when logical thinking isn't giving you the answers you need.

Are you struggling with a decision or problem? Write it down and make a request to your subconscious to come back to you with an answer within a specific time frame – the next day, in two days or even a week. And then leave it. Go for a walk, take a bath, sleep on it.

Then come back and consider it again. A fresh mind will give you a new perspective. (And if it doesn't, don't get stressed, simply repeat the process until it does. Because it will.)

WALK

"Methinks that the moment my legs begin to move, my thoughts begin to flow."

HENRY DAVID THOREAU

When you go for a walk, your heart pumps faster, circulating more blood and oxygen not just to the muscles but to all the organs – including the brain. Many experiments have show that after exercise, even very mild exercise such as walking, people perform better on tests of memory and attention.

Walking at your own pace also creates a connection between your body rhythm and the rhythm of your mind. Your attention is free to wander and this kind of mental state is strongly associated with having innovative ideas and strokes of insight.

Don't take your phone, don't count your steps,
just walk and let your mind wander.

COLOURING

Do you want to feel calmer and more focused?
Would you like to boost your creativity? Spend
five minutes in the morning colouring.

NOT KNOWING

"In the beginner's mind there are many possibilities, in the expert's mind there are few."

SHUNRYU SUZUKI

Certainty is reassuring but being uncertain is how we learn; not knowing is what drives progress, after all. Being comfortable with not knowing makes us more open to the world and enables us to fully embrace its possibilities, but learning to be happy with the unknown takes practice. This exercise is designed to help you see the things you don't know as opportunities rather than something to be wary of.

Write down ten things you don't know or don't understand –
anything from how to get jam to set to black holes. Make finding
out more about these things one of your goals for the year.

BRAIN TEASERS

It is possible to try too hard, especially when you're wrestling with a difficult decision, or searching for a solution to a complex problem. At times like these, it is important to remember that the answer is there.

Our brains are brilliant at seeing patterns, both in the physical environment and our inner life, and brain games are an excellent way of tapping into this ability. Try these morning brain teasers and then see what pops into your head later in the day.

1 Arrange ten coins like this on a table:

Can you move just two coins to form two symmetrical lines, each consisting of six coins?

Continued ⟶

BRAIN TEASERS

2 Recite the days of the week backward and then in alphabetical order.

3 Add up the sum of your birthday, dd/mm/yyyy. Now try your partner's, children's, best friend's.

4 Name two objects for every letter of your name. Repeat daily, increasing (and changing) the number of objects each time.

5 Make a matchstick grid like this:

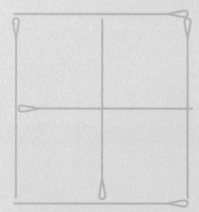

Move two matchsticks to create six squares.

6 Draw a map of your neighbourhood, including as many streets and landmarks as you can. Give yourself five minutes to complete it.

NOTICE YOUR DREAMS

---

*"I am a daydreamer
and a night-thinker."*

UNKNOWN

Much of what we dream is simply noise, no more than a collection
of random images that our brains have collected during the day.
But humans are past masters at self-deception and, because our
subconscious minds become active when we sleep, it is possible
that our dreams have something to tell us.

Try keeping a dream journal by your bed. Write down everything you remember when you wake up, recording what happened exactly as you remember it, regardless of how little sense it seems to make. Look back over it every few days; don't be too analytical, just treat these dreams as things to explore rather than be solved, and be alert to recurring themes.

DREAM SYMBOLS

Falling relates to letting go, which may trigger anxiety. It may also relate to fear of failure or fear of losing control.

Water is a symbol of the unconscious mind, the state of the water reflecting your state of mind. So a calm lake will symbolize a calm, clear mind while rough seas will reflect unease.

Dreaming that you are naked is related to the sense that you are somehow revealing yourself to others. It might be a sign of feeling vulnerable or conversely that you desire more recognition.

Missing a flight, train or important meeting in your dream can be connected with making a big decision and worrying about missing opportunities.

Exams can symbolize self-reflection or self-evaluation, that you are putting a part of yourself under the microscope.

If a road plays a significant part in your dream it may symbolize your "life path" and that you are considering which direction to take.

BOOST YOUR CREATIVITY

Creative thinking plays a key role in problem solving so, whatever we do in our professional lives, we all need to nurture our innate creativity.

Here are some things to try:

- Create a positive environment. Our surroundings have the power to affect our mood and we can't think creatively with a negative mind-set, so make sure your home and/or office lifts your spirits.

- Change your perspective. If you need to come up with a creative solution to a problem, try looking at it from someone else's point of view. How would your partner or best friend approach it; for example?

- Ask "What if...?" Think of a past event and then imagine what would have happened if you had done X instead of Y. How would it have affected the outcome?

- Improvise. Too much pre-planning can hamper creativity. This exercise is designed to help you to think on your feet.

- Go somewhere you know you won't be disturbed and write down three issues that are in the news right now. Close your eyes and pick one. Now talk about that issue for four minutes (set a timer). Don't look anything up, just say whatever comes into your head.

MIND MAPPING

A mind map is a visual representation of your thoughts using associations, connections and triggers to stimulate further ideas. Mind maps mirror your brain's natural way of doing things and can help you solve problems and think more creatively.

Write a topic in the centre of the page, or use an image.

Now draw branches radiating out from this centre point and write a related idea on each.

Add more ideas on sub-branches. Use pictures and colours, key words and symbols – anything that will stimulate your brain.

I AM THE PROBLEM, I AM THE SOLUTION

Sometimes it feels as though life is controlling us, rather than the other way around. When that happens, it's useful to remind ourselves that, while we may not be able to control everything that happens to us, we can control our reactions and responses.

Begin by writing down the thing that's causing you to feel out of control – "I am putting on weight" or "I have too much to do at work", for example.

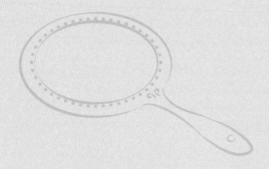

Now make a list of ways you could resolve the situation, beginning each possible solution with the phrase "I can choose". "I can choose to walk home rather than take the bus"; "I can choose to speak to my boss about my workload"; "I can choose to make healthy choices in the supermarket." Say each sentence aloud.

FOCUS ON PRODUCTIVITY

Once you have mental clarity, an understanding of what really matters to you and how to create an attitude of abundance, it is time to sharpen your productivity tools and achieve your dreams and goals.

DON'T WAIT – EAT THE FROG

"If it is your job to eat a frog, it's best to do it first thing in the morning. And if it's your job to eat two frogs, it's best to eat the biggest one first."

MARK TWAIN

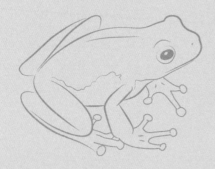

What is the most challenging, but potentially rewarding task that you can do today? Don't put off doing it until the end of the day – you'll just waste time doing less important things and worrying about how you still have to "eat the frog". Write it down. Make it your first task of the day. And then relax.

SETTING AN INTENTION FOR THE DAY

"You are what your deepest desire is. As your desire is, so is your intention. As your intention is, so is your will. As your will is, so is your deed. As your deed is, so is your destiny."

UPANISHADS (CLASSIC AYURVEDIC TEXTS)

Setting an intention is like drawing a map of the route you desire to take. Intentions are not tasks to be accomplished, rather guiding principles for how you want to live and be in the world. Setting intentions is particularly powerful after meditation or when you have simply sat quietly for a few minutes.

Make a list of five intentions, then select one for today. Remember, they must come from the heart, so ask yourself what matters to you most. Keep them positive in tone and write in the present tense.

HOW DO YOU
SPEND YOUR TIME?

"This moment is all there is."

RUMI

While the measurements of time remain the same – the minutes and hours in the day, the weeks and months in the year – how you spend it may change from one day or week or decade to the next.

Just as it is helpful to understand your bigger dreams and priorities, it is also helpful to have a look at how you are regularly spending time on a day-to-day basis.

How did you spend your time yesterday? Write down everything you can think that you did over the course of the day and how long you spent doing it. What were the time-wasters? What would you like to spend more time on? What can you do today to take one step toward spending your time more wisely?

_____

_____

_____

_____

_____

_____

_____

_____

_____

_____

_____

_____

_____

_____

_____

_____

STACK YOUR TASKS

In a professional kitchen, the chefs will prepare their stations meticulously at the beginning of the shift so that they have everything they need within arm's reach, ready to begin service. In this way, they don't need to walk constantly from one end of the kitchen to the other, getting in everyone else's way and slowing down service.

Stacking a series of small tasks or actions together allows you to create a routine, which can then be easily repeated and so making this a really efficient use of your time.

We all have a different combination of tasks that we need to do during the day, but this idea of finding ways to stack them together can be useful and satisfying. Spend five minutes now writing down your ideas for how you can stack your tasks more effectively for the day ahead.

THE POWER OF "NO"

Saying "no" is a way of establishing our boundaries; it is an assertion of ourselves. Most of us were good at it when we were toddlers, obstinately refusing to sit in our push chairs or eat our broccoli but, as adults, we often find it difficult to say "no" because we want to please, we want to be liked and we don't want to cause offence. But saying "yes" to absolutely everything – to always feeding the neighbour's cat, to always joining the fundraising committees, to always staying on at the office – leaves us over-committed, stressed out and feeling a little bit put upon.

The following exercise is designed to help you work out when to sign up and when to just say "no".

Write down the request then divide the rest of the page into three columns. In the left-hand column write the following questions:

- Do I really, in my heart of hearts, want to do this?

- Does what I have been asked to do align with my goals and values?

- Will I feel good doing this?

The next two columns are for your answers – one for "yes", one for "no". Be honest and take your time. If "no" outweighs "yes", then you should politely decline.

ELIMINATE AND DELEGATE

"From a young age, I learned to focus on the things I was good at and delegate to others what I was not good at."

SIR RICHARD BRANSON

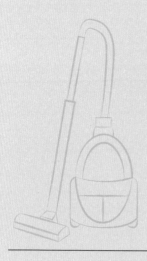

Have a look again at how you spend your time (page 133). Now it's time for the fun part – what could you eliminate from this list and what could you delegate. According to Tim Ferriss, author of *The 4-Hour Work Week*, the best tasks to delegate are those that are "both time-consuming and well-defined". Spend five minutes this morning seeing if you can save yourself an hour a week to start with, an hour you can spend doing something more useful or fun instead.

If you're finding it hard to imagine handing tasks over because you think it's easier just to get things done yourself rather than show others how, don't try to change everything at once. Choose one thing that you can organize handing over today or that you can schedule in time to eliminate.

Eliminate examples:

Schedule 30 minutes a week to unsubscribe from unwanted email marketing.

No more open-ended meetings. Always put a time limit and have an agenda.

Stop having to-do lists all over the house. Designate one place and format.

Delegate examples:

Outsource research.

Delegate household chores, with rewards for everyone (and more time for you).

Ask a friendly school parent to share the school run.

ASK FOR WHAT YOU WANT

Asking for things is a sign that we recognize the importance of our own needs. Good askers are clear about what they want, why they want it and who they want it from. They ask politely and with confidence because they expect a "yes" (although they will also have rationalized a "no", just in case). However, good askers are in a minority. Most of us ask apologetically, if we ask at all.

What can you ask for, today?

Here are some tips for becoming a more effective asker:

- Know exactly what you want. Before you ask, try writing your request down in one simple sentence. Once you are clear about what you want, you will be able to make your request with more confidence.

- Ask the right person. If you are asking for a pay rise, a grant or sponsorship for a charity event then do your research and make sure the person you are asking is in a position to say "yes".

- Be bold. People rarely give you more than you ask for, so think what your ideal would be and ask for it.

- Know why the person you are asking should say "yes". It might help to make a list of the reasons first. Think about each one and ask yourself whether or not it would convince you.

- Be clear. Make your request simply, don't drop hints or wrap it up in thinly veiled criticism. (For example, if you want your partner to come with you to an event just say, "I would love it if you came with me tomorrow," rather than "There's this function after work tomorrow and other people are going with their partners. We never do anything together.")

- Explain what saying "yes" will involve.

- Practise. If you've forgotten how to ask, start small. Try asking someone in the supermarket to reach a packet off a high shelf for example, or go into a café and ask for a glass of tap water.

- Be okay with "no". You need to assume your request will be met, but you also need to know in your own mind that "no" does not spell disaster. A "no" just means nothing has changed. And you can always ask again.

DISTRACTIONS

"To be everywhere is nowhere."

SENECA

Our heads are brim-full of different thoughts, but we can only
properly focus on one thing at a time, which means that all but
one of those thoughts is a distraction.

Ask yourself, "What am I going to achieve today?"

Write the answer down on a piece of paper and stick it somewhere you will be certain to see it. This is your focus for the day. (If you move around a lot, you may need to write it on several different pieces of paper and distribute them throughout your home or office.)

Every time you sense your attention wandering, bring your mind back to your goal.

BE AN EARLY RISER

The theme of this journal is spend just five minutes in the morning each day to reflect, check in with yourself and sharpen your focus for the day ahead. Giving yourself this short period of time will have a direct positive effect on your productivity levels.

If you struggle to look forward to the mornings, here are some tips for how to become a naturally early riser:

Get up at the same time each morning.

Put your alarm clock out of reach so that you have to physically get up to switch it off.

Use the natural daylight to help you wake up by going to the window.

In the evening, get your things together for the morning and practice looking forward to the morning and all the productivity it brings.

Design your own personal morning routine. What does it look like? Do you jump straight into the shower, stretch or sit quietly savouring a cup of tea? What is your ideal everyday breakfast?

FIND YOUR
ONE THING

Most of us have more things to do than we have hours in the day in which to do them. Whether we sink or swim depends on our ability to prioritize and so finding your "one thing" is an effective way to focus on what really matters.

What are the areas in your life where you feel either overwhelmed by your to-do list or that you are never able to give very much attention to?

Work

Home

Relationships

Social life

Health

Finance

Leisure time

Choose one area to consider today.

At the top of the page, write the question "What is the one thing I can do to make this part of my life better/easier/more productive?"

Make it your goal to do whatever you write in response.

_____

_____

_____

_____

_____

_____

_____

_____

_____

_____

_____

_____

_____

_____

_____

_____

_____

_____

HABIT MAKING

Lasting change comes when the new actions, thoughts or behaviours we have decided to adopt become daily habits. But how do we go about making something a habit?

In *The Power of Habit*, Charles Duhigg describes how habits are routines that contain three basic steps; there is a cue that triggers a behaviour that leads to a reward. When you want to change your habits you need to work out how to change the behaviour in the middle of this process rather than the cue or the reward.

For example, if you were someone who suffered from an afternoon dip in energy and your usual pick-me-up was a chocolate bar, rather than trying to ignore the cue of tiredness, you would focus on replacing the chocolate bar with something healthy that has the same effect of waking you up; you could go for a quick walk outside, drink a glass of water or have a cup of green tea.

Here are some ideas:

- Link the new habit to something you already do as part of your everyday routine. For example, if your goal is to lead a more active life and you already go to fetch the papers on a Saturday morning, start walking to the shop instead of driving. Or if you want to achieve a calmer mind and you already take the train to work, start using that time to just sit quietly and focus on your breathing.

- Make it easy. There's no point telling yourself that you are going to run or meditate for an hour every day. You won't. The secret to successful habit forming is to make it so easy that you barely notice. Do some push-ups while the shower water heats up; close your eyes and take three deep breaths while the kettle boils.

- Do it every day.

- Set a specific time and place for this habit.

- Plan for problems ahead. Think about the obstacles that might get in your way and how you will overcome them. For example, if your new habit involves exercising outside, then perhaps you will plan to go the gym when it rains. Or if it takes a big chunk of time, you could devise a shorter version so that you never have to skip the action entirely.

- Be patient and allow yourself to stumble. It takes time for something to become a habit and the world won't end if you miss a day or two. When the stumble happens, and it will, just remind yourself why you are trying to set this habit and pick up where you left off.

- Reward yourself. We are more likely to maintain a habit if we associate the action with a reward. Treat yourself to a soak in the bath after a run; have an extra-large cup of tea in your favourite mug when you've completed your breathing exercise.

- Boost your motivation by writing or voicing affirmations such as "I am doing well making exercise part of my daily routine."

FLOW

Most of us have experienced moments when we are so totally absorbed in an activity that all the stresses and distractions of the day melt away, our minds still and time disappears. Some people refer to these moments as "being in the zone", others say they are in a state of "flow", but whatever the terminology, when you get there, it feels great.

Here are some tips to help you achieve a state of flow.

Do something you enjoy for its own sake rather than for what you achieve by doing it. Lots of people reach a state of flow when they're running, for example, but you will never get there if you only run because it helps you lose weight.

Choose something sufficiently challenging to keep you focused, but not so hard that it requires too much conscious effort. Repetitive tasks such as swimming lengths or colouring work well.

Know why you are doing it – opt for something that aligns with your core goals and values.

Eliminate all other distractions. You will never achieve flow if you are listening for the beep of your distance counter or phone alert so leave all the gadgetry behind.

MONO-TASKING

Concentrating on one thing at a time reduces stress and makes us more productive, but multi-tasking has become so commonplace that many of us rarely give anything our undivided attention.

You don't need to mono-task at all times, but it's a great focus practice to bring into your daily life. You can relax into one activity for a period of time and get into the flow, from cooking a favourite recipe to tackling a big task or issue at work.

In a time of information overload, give your scatter-brain a well-earned break and enjoy the luxury of doing one thing at a time, and doing it really well.

If you are an inveterate multi-tasker, try this simple exercise for five minutes in the morning.

Think of something to do – read a report, listen to the radio, clean out a cupboard – whatever appeals.

Put away your phone and other technological distractions and spend the next five minutes doing that one thing and absolutely nothing else.

FOOD FOR FOCUS

What's for breakfast? Give yourself time to fuel your body and mind first thing and you'll reap the benefits for the rest of the day. Write down your favourite healthy foods and ways you can easily add more to your daily diet. What are you going to eat today?

Eating mindfully will also help your focus for the day. Trying to work or do anything other than eat while you eat is a false economy as you drain the energy needed by your digestion and so you might either feel the effects of indigestion later, be overly tired or not absorb all the nutrients from your meal.

Giving food your attention and gratitude actually means you are less likely to overeat, and you give yourself a break, time to recharge for the rest of the day.

Oats for slow-release energy

Berries for memory

Omega-3 oily fish (salmon, mackerel, sardines) for healthy brain function

Pumpkin seeds, rich in zinc, for thinking

QUITTING

---

*"Of all the stratagems,
to know when to quit is best."*

CHINESE PROVERB

Sometimes the plan doesn't work, no matter how hard we try. Battling
on will simply lower our spirits and use up time that could be better spent
on something else. When that happens, it's time to give up and move on.
Don't look back.

Are you juggling too many balls in the air right now? Would you actually be able to accomplish more if you tried to do a little bit less? Spend a few minutes this morning exploring if you might be better off moving on from a current project.

FINISHING

"I long to accomplish a great and noble task, but it is my chief duty to accomplish small tasks as if they were great and noble."

HELEN KELLER

When you're really close to the finishing line of a task or project, you might need to persevere to finish what you started. Stick to your resolve and remember that it doesn't matter how small or great the task might be, enjoy the accomplishment.

Finishing can be hard and it is all too easy to slip back into your pre-goal state. Here are some suggestions to help you finish successfully.

- Announce it. When you're done, say so. The words will have more impact spoken out loud.

- Stop and enjoy the moment. Achieving your goal, whatever it is, is something to celebrate, so take time to look at the new view.

- Assess and process all that you've learned along the way.

- Thank the people who have helped you get there.

And now go ahead and set a new goal.

ACKNOWLEDGMENTS

Picture credits: Dreamstime.com Yuliya Derbisheva 81; **Shutterstock** Anastasia Nio 69; Azurhino 45; Eisfrei 1, 12, 41, 88, 116, 150, 155; Julia Poleeva 134; krisArt 14; Le Panda 86; Natalia Hubbert 46; ninanaina backgrounds throughout; Silmairel 107; Stefa_Stefo4ka 84; Yuliya Derbisheva 26.

Acknowledgments

p. 32, Copyright © Suzy Kassem, *Rise Up and Salute the Sun* 2011

p. 38, Copyright © The Estate of Elizabeth David, *At Elizabeth David's Kitchen Table* 2010

p. 54, Copyright © Elizabeth Gilbert, *On Being* podcast with Krista Tippett 7 July 2016

p. 64, Copyright © Oprah Winfrey, *Personal Mission Statements of 5 Famous CEOs (And Why You Should Write One Too)*, Stephanie Vozza, *Fast Company* 2014

p. 64, Copyright © Stephen R Covey, *The 7 Habits of Highly Effective People* 1989, 2004

p. 82, Copyright © Roy Bennett, *The Light in the Heart* 2016

p. 138, Copyright © Richard Branson, *Like a Virgin: Secrets They Won't Teach You at Business School* 2012

p. 139, Copyright © Charles Duhigg, *The Power of Habit: Why We Do What We Do in Life and Business* 2012

p. 148, Copyright © Tim Ferris, *The 4-Hour Work Week: Escape the 9-5, Live Anywhere and Join the New Rich* 2007

Contributor: Charlotte Abrahams

Consultant Publisher: Kate Adams

Editorial Assistant: Nell Warner

Copyeditor: Jane Birch

Senior Designer: Jaz Bahra

Designer & Illustrator: Ella McLean

Picture Library Manager: Jen Veall

Picture Research Manager: Giulia Hetherington

Production Controller: Beata Kibil